WHAT HAPPENS WHEN YOU MEET YOU?

What Happens When You Meet You?

FRED RENICH

TYNDALE HOUSE
PUBLISHERS,
Wheaton, Illinois

Scripture quotations are from the *American Standard Version* (© by International Council of Reli-
gious Education, 1929) and are reprinted with per-
mission of Thomas Nelson & Sons.

Library of Congress Catalog Card Number
77-52045
ISBN 0-8423-7875-8
What happens When You Meet You? was originally
   published by Living Life Publications, Mont-
   rose, Pennsylvania.
First printing, February, 1978
Printed in the United States of America

TO
MY DARLING
JILL
WHO BY HER EXAMPLE
AND ENCOURAGEMENT
HAS HELPED ME LEARN TO
ACCEPT MYSELF

Contents

Introduction

Perhaps no fear is more prevalent nor more devastating than the fear of failure. In the degree to which a person is involved in a success oriented society, fear of failure is compounded.

There is a counterpart to secular success for dedicated Christians. In this group success is measured in two dimensions: time and

/or results in Christian service and depth of personal Christian experience.

Failure in either of these areas, whether real or imagined, has immeasurable negative repercussions for the person who drinks that bitter cup. The fear of failure is for the Christian oftentimes more intolerable than that experienced by his secular counterpart.

For sixteen years I concentrated on working closely with young Christian workers, most of whom were under appointment to various mission posts around the world.

One of the most helpful subjects discussed with these people centered around the implications of an almost universal fear of failure, with the corresponding difficulty of being composed about one's weaknesses.

This first volume in *The Christian Development Series* deals with this crucial issue. It is based on the premise that we have no right to reject what God has accepted, to hate what He loves, or to treat as worthless something for which He has paid an infinite price. God considers man to be infinitely valuable!

I am particularly indebted to my wife Jill, who for more than thirty years has encouraged me to have a positive attitude toward myself, even in those many situations when my weaknesses, failures and sins seemed inundating in their impact.

Who can measure the value of grown children who have added their encouragement by constantly demonstrating confidence in their dad? Without the urgings of such a loyal family this book would not have been written.

In addition I want to express appreciation to the many Christian workers who have urged me to put into print the substance of our many discussions on the general subject of Self Acceptance.

My heartfelt thanks to our daughter Jan Barger who typed the manuscript and assisted in editorial and proof-reading tasks. And my deep appreciation to Anne Whitney who has given so generously and enthusiastically of her time and talent in designing the book and illustrating the text.

Fred. C. Renich
March, 1975

Chapter One
Running Scared

She was an attractive college girl—good family background—outgoing personality—a girl with vibrant health, good looks, and one who gave every evidence of a young lady enjoying life to the fullest.

"Mr. Renich, if people knew who I really am they wouldn't want to be around me!"

Pam had come to see me after a meeting in her church and something I said enabled her to open up. After her initial statement she poured out the all too familiar story of a normal person who, along life's highway, had hit a patch of ice and wound up in a heap on the median strip.

Behind the front door of nearly every life are the hidden secrets, the carefully guarded realities that we all fear having exposed even to close friends or loved ones.

But there is a deeper kind of personal hiddenness which is much more devastating. Many of us try to hide even from ourselves. To keep things away from the eyes of a gazing public may be justified, but why should we run scared from ourselves?

The Apostle Paul, writing to the Roman Christians in verse three of chapter twelve says:

"For I say, through the grace that was given me, to every man that is among you, not to think of himself more highly than he ought to think; but so to think as to think soberly, according as God hath dealt to each man a measure of faith."

Paul gives us a tough assignment. We are supposed to THINK—

— about ourselves
— realistically, or honestly
— according to a certain yardstick or evaluating measure—faith!

You are to think about you, and I am to think about me—honestly. Strangely enough in my experience of working with hundreds of earnest Christians over a period of years, I have found it is exceedingly difficult for Christians to be *wholesomely honest with themselves about themselves*. A direct result of this is an inability to be really honest with others. Parents don't tell their children the truth, husbands shade the truth with their wives, and wives aren't open with their husbands.

One day I met with a small group of

Christian workers for a time of discussion. The leader began by asking each of us to jot down four things we WANTED people to know about us.

Wow! That was tough!

I really struggled over that!

I felt foolish, embarrassed, and in a corner.

There were many things that secretly I admired in myself that I really wanted others to know about. But to put them on paper and then to read them to the group was almost worse than confessing my sins!

Now why should anyone object to telling the truth about what he felt were his good points?

Try the little exercise for yourself. Take just a minute or two and jot down on a scrap of paper four things that you really want people to know about you. Avoid generalities, spiritual cliches, or the Christian witness phrases, like—"I want everyone to know I love Jesus," or "I want people to know I'm a Christian."

I was the director of a Christian organization at the time and the discussion was taking place in our office. Guess what I wanted people to know about me? Over in the corner of the room was a plant, a poinsettia in bloom. I had grown it from cutting to flower—and I wanted people to know that. But it was tough putting it down on paper.

Try the same exercise on your friends or your family. Then discuss the whole thing with them. Did any of you find it difficult? Why? Or maybe for you it was easy. If so, why?

Why do we find it hard to be honest?

Why do we run scared?

Because each of us feels he hasn't measured up!

But to what?

Have you thought through what you feel you are to measure up to? Most of us have a vague sense of idealism and the feeling that we are falling short haunts us.

Even in what we want people to know about us we hesitate. Do we feel they are not worth the importance we put on them? After all, should the director of a missionary training organization be proud of growing a little thing like a poinsettia? He should want people to know something really important about him—like being a very sacrificial Christian, or some other trait that fits the spiritual image!!

The feeling of being bound to the ideal varies from person to person, but it's a part of every person's make-up. That is good. But he is not to be a slave to it.

Another reason it's hard to be honest is our concept of humility. After all doesn't Romans 12:3 say we are not to think of ourselves more highly than we ought to think? Isn't that a command to be humble?

Not really. It's rather a command to be realistic—honest—genuine. The verse also implies we aren't to think too lowly of ourselves.

Looking at the verse superficially many of us have gone to an extreme. We have concentrated on maintaining a low degree of self-esteem. But to be too negative about one's self is just as bad or worse than being overly positive. After all false humility is just a reverse form of pride. Some people are proud of their nothingness.

This tendency to false humility is supported by a whole array of excellent hymns, lots of misunderstood theology, and plenty of zealous and earnest preaching.

A standard assignment I used with missionary candidates was a very simple one, but for many it proved to be a traumatic experience. Each person was asked to compile

a list of his strengths and weaknesses. They
were to make two columns:

STRENGTHS   WEAKNESSES

_____   _____

_____   _____

_____   _____

_____   _____

Under each strength and weakness they
were to list two recent incidents or experience that supported their evaluation of themselves.

The difficulty many had handling this
fairly simple assignment is evidence that
many Christians, including Christian workers, are "running scared".

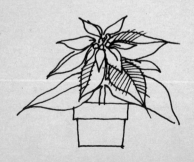

Chapter Two
Who Are You?

Do you realize you're really two people? The external visible person everyone can see and the inner hidden person very few people see. In fact this "internal person" is often hidden even from you!

Many who don't think they are "running scared" are still strangers to their real selves.

How can you find out who you really are? One simple way is to start paying attention to the way you react to individual life situations. Only living people react to life. You can do what you want with a corpse. It just lies there. But try punching a living person in the nose. You'll have a problem on your hands!

We were going through a famous museum in London, England where the historical figures on display were made of wax. I got lost and turned to a guard to ask directions. He didn't reply—he was a piece of wax! I reacted, he didn't. I got red in the face and embarrassed—he just stood there!

Study the diagram below:

1. The circle represents the outer, exterior you. The you everyone sees.
2. The interior hidden you is represented

by the figure at the center of the circle.
3. Arrows from the outside and pointing toward the circle are individual life situations.
4. Arrows from the center and pointing toward the outside are your specific reactions to your life situations.

Note that the reaction arrows vary in length. This is to convey the fact that your reactions vary in expression, degree and duration. Some are extremely vivid. Others barely break through the level of your consciousness (the rim of the circle).

Life comes to you one circumstance at a time, though these circumstances come with almost lightening rapidity and they keep coming constantly. To each individual circumstance there is a reaction.

Your reactions vary. Some are so vivid, intense and sufficiently strong they make lasting impressions on your memory: the deep sorrows, exhilarating joy, bitter disappointment or unchangeable tragedy. Other reactions barely break the circle of consciousness. There are myriads of these for each of the more vivid ones.

IT IS THESE REACTIONS TO LIFE THAT EXPRESS THE REAL YOU!

The difficulty is that you tend to ignore, suppress or forget many of your less vivid reactions and even many of the vivid ones you'd probably like to forget.

If you are to know who you really are, you need to begin taking notice of all your reactions, the seemingly insignificant as well as the vivid, important ones.

Try a simple exercise:

Pause now and make a list of all the reactions you can think of that occured during the last two or three days. Describe each one in a couple of words if possible, like:

worried	calm	covetous
excited	upset	lustful
happy	irritated	angry
indifferent	fearful	compassionate
tense		

Don't try to evaluate or justify them now. Just note what they are.

Next, study the following scriptures:

Mark 7:21, 22: "For from within, out of the heart of men, evil thoughts proceed, fornication, thefts, murders, adulteries, covetings, wickednesses, deceit, lasciviousness, an evil eye, railing, pride, foolishness."

Galatians 5:17-19: "Now the works of

the flesh are manifest, which are these: fornication, uncleanness, lasciviousness, wraths, factions, divisions, parties, envyings, drunkenness, revellings, and such like. . . ."

Galatians 5:22: *"But the fruit of the Spirit is love, joy, peace, longsuffering, kindness, goodness, faithfulness, meekness, self-control. . . ."*

Colossians 3:5-15: *"Put to death therefore your members which are upon the earth: fornication, uncleanness, passion, evil desire, and covetousness, which is idolatry . . . but now do ye also put them all away: anger, wrath, malice, railing, shameful speaking out of your mouth: lie not one to another; . . . (but) put on . . . a heart of compassion, kindness, lowliness, meekness, longsuffering; forbearing one another, and forgiving each other, if any man have a complaint against any; even as the Lord forgave you, so also do ye . . . put on love . . . let the peace of Christ rule in your hearts . . . and be ye thankful."*

I Corinthians 13:4-8: *"Love suffereth long and is kind; love envieth not; love vaunteth not itself, is not puffed up, doth not behave itself unseemly, seeketh not its own, is not provoked, taketh not account of evil; rejoiceth not in unrighteousness, but rejoiceth with the truth; beareth all things, be-*

lieveth all things, hopeth all things, endureth all things. Love never faileth . . ."

Divide the descriptive terms in these Scriptures into two lists: negative and positive and/or wholesome and unwholesome.

Now look at the lists you have made of your own reactions.

Consolidate them.

Divide them into negative and positive, or wholesome and unwholesome categories.

See if there is any similarity between your reactions and those listed in the Bible verses you have studied.

Be as honest and as objective as you can in this exercise. You need to know *who* you really are, whether the picture is good and pleasant or otherwise. You may find it difficult and frightening to look at the real you. Don't let that bother you. Many people hesitate to face the truth about their health. But we can get nowhere by hiding from ourselves, building fences, wearing masks, or in a variety of ways, "running scared". You *must* face the facts about the real you. To do so you must know *who you really are*.

Chapter Three
The Dilemma

There are at least three stubborn realities you automatically face when you begin being honest about who you are.

1. God is holy—unchangeably so!
2. Your conscience tells you God condemns that in you which is wrong, and that if you aren't condemning yourself, you ought to be.
3. People will or ought to condemn you.

Depending on the strength with which you are alive to these three realities you will probably have difficulty being inwardly free in looking at the real you.

For the sincere Christian, the fact of God's holiness is the most difficult of the three realities with which to cope. But the other two also can be exceedingly difficult.

Guilt makes us try to hide from our real selves so we resort to a variety of superficially effective techniques for reconciling the holiness of God with our own sinfulness.

Most of these take the form of various escapist mental positions:

"Oh well, other good Christians are doing it, so why worry?"

"After all, it was the other person's fault."

"You can't expect to be perfect."

"Since I'm righteous *in Christ* (positionally holy), my behaviour doesn't need to be all that good."

"It's wonderful that God looks at my robe of imputed righteousness, not at the real me."

"Oh well, I guess I'm just a carnal Christian. I'll probably not get very many rewards if I keep on this way, but at least I'll be saved, and that's what's important."

"Those bad reactions are the "old man" part of me—like Paul in Romans 7. Since *he* had a problem, I guess I'm not really too bad."

The kind of justifying rationalization you use depends on your particular theological background, and may vary from the above illustrations, but in any case your mental position takes some form of *rejecting or hiding from the real person you know yourself to be.*

Usually there is a great deal of personal guilt attached to this rejection.

BUT TO ACCEPT OURSELVES *AS WE ARE* WOULD ONLY INCREASE THE GUILT—OR SO WE THINK!!

Chapter Four

Finding
The Answer

When I talked to the college girl mentioned in Chapter One, I took Pam mentally out to the freeway. It was winter with patches of ice here and there on the pavement. As I pictured rounding a curve, there in the median strip was what had once been a beautiful Cadillac. It was now a pile of twisted wreckage.

"What a horrible automobile," I exclaimed. "You'll never catch me buying a Cadillac! Any car that can get messed up like that shouldn't even be sold."

Pam looked puzzled. What was I talking about?

"It wasn't the Cadillac's fault that it got messed up. Why blame the car when obviously it was the driver's fault?" she mused.

I let her think for a bit then made the point.

"It wasn't the car but the control package that was responsible. The driver wasn't able to handle the auto at the speed he was driving with ice on the curve."

Pam began to see it. She was condemning and rejecting herself instead of recognizing the fact that her control was inadequate for the circumstances in which she had found herself.

MAN'S FAULTY CONTROL SYSTEM

Man is the only one of God's creatures who doesn't have a built-in automatic control system. The members of the animal world operate on a built-in instinctual control mechanism. They do what they do because they are programmed that way. You can't feed a pig to death (we use self-feeders for them), but man will dig his grave with his teeth. Sexual deviancy is rare in the animal world but bestiality (humans cohabiting with animals) is not uncommon among people. Birds fly south in the autumn and north in the spring, and they don't fly east or west.

Who taught them to navigate? They are programmed to do it.

Man on the other hand, endowed as he is by a fantastic set of internal dynamics: mind, will, emotion, appetite, life-drives; remains without a control system. God intended to be his control. And when in the Garden of Eden man declared his independence from God, he was left to the tyranny of his own inner drives, emotions, appetites, mind and will.

But these dynamics were intended to be

his servants under a control by God and which was to operate through man's dependency relationship to Him.

Did you ever notice how small a match it takes to light a blazing bonfire? In the same way such seemingly trivial matters act as matches to light the powder kegs of our own nature.

The problem does not lie in our nature, but in the absence of God as its only adequate control dynamic.

". . . it is not in man that walketh to direct his steps." (Jeremiah 10:23)

When we fail to distinguish between what we are as persons and the fact of inadequate control we get into serious trouble. We start thinking of our God-given endowments as evil in themselves instead of seeing that the evil comes from the way these endowments are used. Appetite for food is God-given and is good in itself. But the wrong use of appetite makes it a channel for evil. Gluttony, which is sin, is just a wrong use of a God-given desire for food which is good and necessary. Sex is a good wholesome and God-given drive. But when used wrongly it occasions sin.

When Pam saw that her improper behaviour did not mean that she was herself evil and therefore to be rejected, she had taken the first major step toward recovery.

ACCEPTANCE DOES NOT MEAN APPROVAL

We further complicate our problem by assuming that God's acceptance of us implies His approval of all that we are. We follow this by feeling that our acceptance of ourselves means we approve of that within us which is wrong. In both cases we place ourselves in an impossible position.

Something within us recoils at the idea of a holy God approving obvious evil. We also find it impossible to be self-respecting and at the same time approve of known evil in our lives.

But acceptance does not necessarily imply approval. Rather, acceptance *involves purpose*. God loves a fallen world and He has accepted it—not to approve it, but to redeem it. He *loves and accepts* sinful man *with a view to redeeming him*.

As a boy in high school I enrolled in a course in beginning typing. I knew nothing about the course or the art of using such a mysterious machine. The teacher *did not* spend three days or even one minute scolding me for my stupidity about typewriters or typing. She had accepted me into the class *with a purpose*. In a very real sense she did not approve of her pupil's ignorance. That's why she was in the business of teaching people to type.

All progress in any area of life must begin from where you are. You never start from where you could have been or should be.

We know this, but it's so difficult to accept it and live it.

Rush hour traffic is a fact of life in big cities. Yet how many who get caught in it refuse to accept it. You don't have to approve of it, but you do have to accept it. And to refuse to accept a fact only compounds your problem with it.

Parents know they have to accept their children as they are and work with them at the child's level if real development and improvement are to be realized. And yet how many parents refuse to do this and expect adult performance from a child's mind and body!

The Bible is full of illustrations of the fact that God accepts His broken world *for a purpose*, although He doesn't approve it. In Genesis 3:21-24 we see God working with fallen man—accepting him as he was after his disobedience—with a view to redeeming him.

This acceptance with purpose is seen in the estrangement that occured between Adam and Eve and between man and God. To Adam and Eve, God instituted the permanence of clothing to keep them and us reminded of the barriers to be overcome in establishing true oneness in marriage.* To keep sinful man reminded of his heart estrangement from a holy God, our first parents were driven from the Garden. They were driven

---

*See note at end of chapter.

from God's immediate presence and from all that was implied by residence in that delightful place. The flaming sword of Divine judgment now stands as a permanent barrier between us and God. It forces us to renounce our proud, self-assertive independence and to return to the place of broken, dependent pleading for forgiveness and mercy. There is no other way back into fellowship with the Holy One.

God fully accepted man's fallen condition with all of its terrible effects on man himself and his relationships. But His acceptance had with it a glorious purpose—*man's total redemption.*

Only as you start where you are, fully accepting yourself as you are, can you start to become what you should be. You also must believe that God accepts you where you are and that He is working to make you what by His grace you can become.

HONESTY

How much did God pay for you?

You admit, don't you, that you were purchased with a price?

How much?

What was it? $5.00, $5,000 or $5,000,-000?

You are saying, "Don't be silly. You can't figure in dollars the value of the life of God's son. Doesn't it say in I Peter 1:18, 19 that we were ". . . redeemed, not with corruptible things, with silver or gold, from your vain manner of life handed down from your fathers; but with precious blood, as of a lamb without blemish and without spot, even the blood of Christ".

You are dead right. The price God paid for you and me is way beyond monetary value. In fact it's in a different value realm altogether. But I want to ask you a question:

"Since when does anyone pay that kind of money for junk?"

Unless it's redeemable!

Unless it has potential!

So, what does that say about you?

You have potential! You are redeem-able!

Did you ever stop to think about what sin really is? Every sin you can think of is only distorted, twisted good. When Satan seduced our first parents and thereby brought sin into the world, he didn't inject something new or foreign into the scheme of things. He only twisted that which was already there and which was good.

Man's relation to God became fouled up.

His values were twisted.

Appetite became master instead of servant.

Love was corrupted by being turned inward toward self instead of remaining outward toward others.

Faith (believing God is good) was distorted into unbelief (believing God is evil).

But because you are redeemable, God hasn't rejected you.

How dare you reject yourself?!

Did God know what He was getting when He purchased you? Did He buy you with His eyes shut?

Be careful about answering that question. If you admit that God bought you with the full knowledge of what you really are, then it follows that *He loves the real you*.

If God loves the real you, have you any right to hate you?

It's amazing how inconsistent we are. We keep telling ourselves and others that God loves sinners. Then we turn right around and hate and reject the first sinner we meet —ourselves!

You have to be honest about what God thinks about you. It's obvious there's a lot of thinking on this score that sounds really great spiritually but at root it's just not realistic.

You must be honest about WHAT YOU THINK OF GOD REGARDING HIS RELATIONSHIP TO THE REAL YOU. i.e., How do you think God *acts* toward you when you let down your hair and are truly yourself?

Do you feel He can love you *only to the degree that your behaviour is acceptable to Him?*

While you admit (mentally) that Jesus lives in your heart, do you feel subconsciously that when you sin Jesus sort of goes back to heaven for a time?

Do you find it difficult to be joyful and full of praise immediately after confessing your sin (right after committing it) and claiming His forgiveness and cleansing? Why does it take a day or two or three to "feel better" after committing a sin? Is God's forgiveness any more real days after you've sinned than it is (or should be) immediately after repentance, confession and accepting His pardon?

Let's get your attitude toward Christ's forgiveness right out into the open. Look at it as it really is. Why carry a vague undefined feeling of remorse, self-reproach, or guilt?

Part of the reason for your inability to *accept* God's forgiveness immediately is this failure to recognize and believe that acceptance and approval are *two different things*. We discussed this earlier but it also applies in this context.

Acceptance of us by God is *not* synonymous with God's approval of us. He can accept what He can't approve *because He plans to change it*. But He can't work on it to change it before He accepts it!

There is also a psychological factor in the problem of accepting immediate forgiveness the moment you sin. If at the time you sinned you are aware of a holy God's hatred of your sin, your feelings of personal guilt can be very strong. And if at that moment you also believe God has to some degree left you, a subtle sense of satisfaction is felt because you feel you are getting what you deserve! You feel it would be wrong *not* to be miserable! You allow yourself to indulge in your miseries because through this you subconsciously achieve a degree of self-atonement, though you wouldn't admit for the world that *this* was your motive.

It's really easier to suffer awhile in the misery of self-reproach, remorse and self-rejection than it is to choose deliberately to believe God forgives you as completely the moment you repent and trust Him as He does after you have suffered for a time and then decide to trust.

In addition to this there is the obvious fact that you feel more keenly about things close to you than when they are removed by the distance of space or time. Three days after you have blown your stack the incident isn't nearly as vivid and the guilt feelings aren't as keen. So it seems easier to trust God for forgiveness and believe He accepts you, not because your faith is stronger, but because the intensity of the issue has diminished.

It is usually much easier to trust God about incidents and issues that aren't right in front of us.

---

*When Eve responded to temptation in the garden she stepped into a new and devastating way of life. Her actions were the result of deception, minimizing her guilt. But Adam acted deliberately and with full knowledge of what he was doing. For him therefore the guilt was complete.

Both Adam and Eve moved—
* from dependence to independence.
* from self-giving to self-getting.
* from being bound together as a cohesive unit to two separate individuals who:
  — acted with self-interest as their motivation instead of the total good as their purpose.
  — acted in disobedience to God.
  — acted in self-assertion for what each wanted.

What were clothes for?

Short-range: For Adam and Eve personally clothes were the external expression of a deeper internal reality— a barrier separating them from each other internally, and which could be overcome only by redeeming love.

Long-range: With sin (selfishness) a part of the human make-up, social relationships needed the external protection of clothing as an enforcement of the fact that hetero-sexual possession was to be limited to marriage. In a society without sin this would be unnecessary. Nudity is forbidden in Scripture and exposure to the opposite sex is permitted only within the sacredness of marriage.

Self-giving visually, bodily, sexually and psychologically are to be acts of love between lawful spouses by which they experience and express the reality of their oneness in each other. As the Bible says: ". . . the two shall become one flesh". (Ephesians 5:30)

Chapter Five
Faith Is The Key

Romans 12:3 states that you are to think of yourself honestly according to a certain criteria. That measuring rod is FAITH. It is TRUST. You are to think of yourself *ac-*

cording to the degree of faith God has given you.

Put differently, that verse says you are to think of yourself honestly according to the degree that your faith (trust) is real, operating, or working.

Faith is an active, aggressive attitude of the mind and will. It expects! It is assurance that what is expected *will* happen. "Now faith is the assurance of things hoped for . . ." Hebrews 11:6. It is more than hoping; it is expecting! Faith is active—the opposite of being passive.

There is a difference between believing good Bible truths and really trusting God. You can believe many things about God without really counting on Him at all.

The test of whether you are trusting God or not is what you do at that point where you face a negative life situation, for example—temper.

The only place you lose your temper is where your will is crossed. You don't usually get mad in church or when you're asleep—unless the preacher goes too long or a noisy child wakes you up.

You lose your temper out in the rough and tumble of life.

How does faith apply to temper? Study the little sketches below.

Obviously when an immovable force, like rush hour traffic, nasty weather, a stubborn boss, or an unmanageable wife gets in the way of your drive (set of your will) something has to give. Scientists tell us that pressure produces heat, and if an actual irresistable force ever did meet an immovable object there would be immediate disintegration due to the intense heat generated by the pressure.

Temper is simply the "blast off" of emotional "heat" due to the pressure created by someone or some situation getting in your way and refusing to move.

It's at the point of pressure that redemption needs to work—and that is where faith needs to function.

What is faith? It is trust, dependence—counting on someone to do what has been promised.

In the case of the temper illustration, you exercise faith by:

1. Accepting the fact that *you* can't move the hinderance out of your way.
2. Giving the whole situation to God. This

involves being willing to let Him take over the total picture:

a) The hinderance to your drive.

b) Your drive itself.

c) The results of you not achieving the goal toward which you were driving.

3. Expecting God to take the situation into His hands so you no longer need to push.

4. Waiting for His directives in the situation. These may say:

a) Wait—until God moves the hindrance.

b) Go back—(choose another goal).

c) Look for an alternate route toward the same goal.

By giving the situation to God with the full expectation that He will undertake in the matter in this way, you have automatically released the tension producing the heat. Emotion has cooled and you are free to act calmly in a Christ-like way and under His direction.

There is all the difference in the world between dealing with yourself in life situations by faith and dealing with yourself by sheer grit and determination. Applying faith (trust) to your circumstances results in blessing to others and spiritual maturing in your own life. To operate by self-effort (the opposite of trust) results in all kinds of harm to yourself and to others.

You can suppress your temper, but you'll probably pay for it in ulcers for you, resentment or bitterness toward the people involved, and a weakening of your Christian character.

This is what Paul was talking about in Romans 8:13: ". . . but if by the Spirit you put to death the deeds of the body, you shall live."

You and I can deal effectively with our negative reactions in *only one way*: by an attitude of childlike trust—*deliberately expressed at the place and time* where the negative reaction begins to assert itself.

This means you have to be willing to meet God about yourself wherever and whenever you are being the real negative you. It also means walking with God one step at a time, moment by moment, in real life. As you give each negative reaction to Him, fully expecting Him to bring the positive into play, He will actually motivate you to do in the situation that which pleases Him.

Chapter Six

How To Develop Faith

The only way to learn to walk is by walking. You didn't learn by sitting on the floor crying because you couldn't walk. And the first step had to be followed by another—and another—and another—until gradually you became steady on your feet and sure in your stride. In a real sense nobody could teach you to walk. You had to learn it by yourself.

The same is true about faith. You can study all about it, read many books that describe the lives of great men of faith, but in the end you only learn to trust by trusting. As in any other endeavor your first efforts will be halting, uncertain, and mixed with many failures. *But you won't learn to trust any faster than you take steps involving trust.* If you really want to see your faith grow, the following suggestions and exercises will help you.

1. On a separate sheet of paper make a list of what you consider to be your essential strengths and weaknesses.

e.g. *Strengths*   *Weaknesses*

   a.   a.

   b.   b.

   c.   c.

2. Try to think of at least two specific personal experiences for each strength and weakness that validate your evaluation. Indicate these illustrations by a brief notation under each appropriate characteristic.

e.g. *Strengths*

   a. Patient—Didn't get uptight when hubby was late for dinner yesterday.

      Was sweet all evening last week when Sue was so crabby for no seeming reason.

Weaknesses

a. Emotionally cold—

Didn't feel any empathy with Dave when he was heartbroken because he was turned down for football.

Every time Mary cries, I feel like tuning her out.

3. Using a concordance or your reference Bible, try to find at least one Scripture reference for each item on your list that supports your decision that the item is a strength or weakness. Jot down the reference next to the item referred to.

e.g. *Strengths*

Patient—Galatians 5:22

Hardworking—Proverbs 22:9

Kind—Proverbs 31:26

Weaknesses

Indecisive—I Kings 18:21

Too work-centered—Luke 10:40, 41

Reluctant to discipline—Proverbs 13:24

4. Now study both lists and see where you can find some correlation between strengths and weaknesses.

a) Can you see that your strengths automatically are a basis for weakness?

e.g.—A hard working person is often

so taken up with his work that he has little time for people and their needs.

b) Do you see that each weakness *can be an opportunity* for you to trust Jesus Christ to transform that weakness into a strength?

In this way you can see your liabilities as potential assets!

This is very important because you naturally tend to emphasize the negatives, which makes it harder to trust without adding to the difficulty by constant negative thinking. e.g.—The fact that you have a temper is evidence that you have drive. Christ wants to bring your drive under control so it can be directed toward achieving useful objectives. Without His control your drive is dissipated in emotional explosions. Gunpowder needs to be restrained and its explosive force directed if it is to do more than make a big flash when ignited.

c) For each weakness find a promise in the Bible that gives you a basis for believing God can and will enable you to overcome that particular negative behavior pattern.

e.g.—Suppose your weakness is a cold, hard heart toward God. How about a promise like Ezekiel 36:26?

5. Choose one weakness (only one) and list as many practical steps as you can think of that might help to correct it. (In addition to prayer and trusting the Lord).

e.g.—Indecisive:

a) Identify the major areas where you have trouble making up your mind.

b) List what you believe are the main reasons for being indecisive.

e.g.—(1) Afraid of making a mistake due to others being critical of me.

      (2) Don't take time to think the issue through, so put off the decision.

      (3) Too idealistic.

      (4) Don't want to commit myself.

      (5) Won't take the time needed to make a decision.

      (6) Afraid of my own judgment.

c) Talk the problem over with your husband or wife or someone close to you.

d) Narrow your concentration down to just one area—e.g.—planning a meal.

e) Give yourself a time limit to plan meals for one day.

f) When you make the decision write it down.

g) Refuse to second-guess or rehash the decision.

6. Write down when (date or time of day) you plan to start putting these steps into practice.

7. Go back to the promise that relates to this weakness. (e.g.—indecisiveness—James 1:5-7)

- * Does God mean what He says?
- * Do you believe He *means it for you in your situation?*

8. Note *when* this weakness (or sin) usually occurs.
   - * Under what circumstances?
   - * Watch for it to show up!

9. When it shows up *you must choose right then* to give the whole situation to God and *expect Him* to fulfill His promise.

10. As you trust Him, and while facing the situation which you have now given consciously to God, step out *in obedience* and *do* what you believe is right.

    e.g.—Suppose you are a chronic worrier. You are expecting God to set you free. Now you are facing something that starts your mind down that same old worry trail. *As you trust*, you MUST deliberately turn your mind away from the worry:
    - * Leave the issue in God's hands.
    - * Think about something else.
    - * Get busy *doing* whatever you ought to be doing at that time.
    - * If there's nothing needing to be done, find something. This will help re-direct your mind.

11. If you can't trust God in the situation and about the weakness or besetting sin *be honest and tell God so.* Don't be afraid. You now have an additional problem—that of unbelief. And you'll have to trust Him about that as well!!
Remember—the measure of your spiritual stature is NOT your—

> Abilities
> Gifts
> Strength of personality
> Dedication
> Determination
> *Amount of time* you spend in prayer
> Faithfulness in Bible reading or study
> Christian activity
> Faithful church attendance
> Degree of acceptable behavior
> Soul winning
> ETC . . .

But—

You are measured by the degree to which YOU LIVE YOUR LIFE DAILY ON THE BASIS OF SIMPLE TRUST.

"This is the work of God, that you *believe*

(continually exercise confidence) in Him (Jesus Christ) whom He (God) hath sent". John 6:29

Your problem, (and mine) is our innate, spontaneous INDEPENDENCE OF GOD.

Redemption brings us back to a growing, HABITUAL DEPENDENCE (TRUST) IN GOD.

Only *weak* people lean—Nobody wants to be weak.

Only *lost* people ask for directions—Nobody wants to be lost.

Only *tired* people need rest—Nobody wants to be tired.

Only *hungry* people need food—Nobody wants to be hungry.

Only *thirsty* people need drink—Who wants to be thirsty?

Only *guilty* people need pardon—Who wants to be guilty?

Only *helpless* people need care and protection—Who wants to be helpless?

Don't be afraid to be any of these. Where your strength ends, God's begins.

Start *today* to learn to walk by faith.

You learn to walk *only* by taking steps.

Even the longest journey is traveled one step at a time.

What's bothering you now?

Take a step of practical trust now, this minute. And remember, we have God's sure promise in Isaiah 49:23:

". . . they that wait for me (put their trust in me) shall not be put to shame."

Chapter Seven
Conclusion

What really happens when you meet you?

Do you run scared?

Avoid yourself—hide—cover up?
Are you *afraid* of what people will find out?

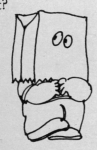

Are you putting on a false front—like big talk—bravado—loud clothes?

Or retreating into a hidden world of day-dreams, make-believe, or just silence? Or

again, maybe burying yourself in an avalanche of activity—busyness—hard work?

You don't need to do any of these.

God isn't in a panic about you. He knows you completely, loves you fully, and is just waiting for you to stop, turn around and say to yourself:

"Hello me!"

"Let's walk together."

"Sure, we've stacks of problems."

"But that's why Christ bought *me*—

—and accepted what He bought—

—and came to live in the wreck of the "house" He purchased . . .

IN ORDER TO DO A FANTASTIC RE-MODELING JOB!"

"But He can't do it while I'm running—because He can only work with the real me that functions out in life at the time and place where I'm being *who* and *what* I really am."

So—

Relax!

Choose today to be free with yourself about yourself.

Since God loves and accepts the real you (with purpose), decide to love and accept the very same person, the real you.

Start *thanking God* that your weaknesses are no longer liabilities!

Thank God they can be assets!

They are opportunities for Him to demonstrate His redeeming love and power.

And each new day—first off—and again and again through each day:

1. Deliberately thank God for Himself *and* for yourself.
2. Tell Him you *are expecting* Him to "come good" in relation to the sins, weaknesses, and mistakes which you freely admit are a part of the *you* He came to save.
3. Tell Him—"Thank you, Lord, for me, a person whom you love—and for whom you have a glorious purpose." Tell Him you *are expecting today's part of that purpose to be fulfilled.*
4. Ask for and accept from Him forgiveness for the many times you have wished you were someone else. Tell Him you *now gladly accept you* as a unique person, intended by Him to fulfill a purpose in His mysterious plan which *no other person can fulfill.*

"Know ye not that your body is the temple of the Holy Spirit?" I Corinthians 6:19

SINCE HE, THE HOLY SPIRIT OF GOD,
IS CONTENT TO LIVE IN YOU—THEN—

HALLELUJAH—

YOU ARE HAPPY TO LIVE THERE
WITH HIM!!!

Aren't you?

TRY IT!!